Father Huddleston's PICTURE BOOK

KLIPTOWN BOOKS
LONDON

Photographs are courtesy of IDAF photolibrary and Bailey's African Photo Archives.

Published in 1990 by Kliptown Books Ltd.
Canon Collins House, 64 Essex Road, London N1 8LR.

British Library Cataloguing in Publication Data

Huddleston, Trevor 1913 –
    Father Huddleston's Picture Book.
    1. Church of England. Huddleston, Trevor 1913 –
    I. Title
    283.092

    ISBN   1-871863-03-1

Printed in England by A. G. Bishop & Sons Ltd,
Orpington, Kent

NOTE

The text in this book was not written but spoken. In other words it is the actual text of the interview for a recent film about me called Makhalipile - The Dauntless One. There is a big difference between writing and speaking, but I think the combination of this text with the remarkable pictures really enhance the value of the book itself. At least I hope so.

Trevor Huddleston

EARLY YEARS

Hampstead Way –
Huddleston's childhood
home

Like thousands of children who were born before the First World War – and I was born just before it in 1913 – many of us had parents overseas. In fact my own father was in the Indian Navy and was therefore abroad when I was born. I didn't see him until I was seven but that wasn't really a hardship. I was brought up by an aunt and my older sister in Hampstead, just opposite Hampstead Heath. We were very lucky because in those days the roads were not made up and we could go off on to the Heath for picnics and walks quite freely. I can remember those days very well. I can remember, for instance, going out with a nurse and seeing a German Zeppelin making a daylight air raid over

Huddleston's aunt and infant sister

London. And I can remember the sound of the bugles calling 'take cover' and 'all clear'.

So I was a wartime child, but I was also a child of the Raj, you might say, like thousands of other kids, so it wasn't very strange to me that I didn't see my father. He and my mother wrote to each other. Sometimes she had to be with him and later on, when the war came to an end, she would spend more time in England and then go back out to him.

That was my origin. It was a very comfortable life. I think I was fairly well spoilt. I had all the traditional blessings (if they are blessings) of a good education. I can remember going to my dame school, just up the hill, and then moving on to a prep school in Hendon which is now no longer there. Of course, that wasn't such a good experience because just after the

Huddleston's Father

Huddleston's Mother

war food was exceedingly short as we were still under rationing. Nevertheless, I think as a child of seven or eight, and I was seven when I went to school as a boarder, you take things as they come. You are not familiar with anything else, anyhow. I was able to come home for the weekends occasionally.

It was a very happy childhood. It is difficult to express nowadays: people always seem to have deep psychological traumas about neglect, but I never felt that in the least and I really enjoyed my school days. I wasn't a great scholar. I don't think I was distinctive in any kind of way, in fact I'm sure I wasn't, at prep school anyhow. But it was a good time.

I can remember when my father retired. He retired early from the Indian Navy, which he commanded at one time. He really didn't like India because it meant being separated from us, from the family and from his relations, and he also felt the weight of the establishment in India. He felt it was a very artificial life. My mother was very different from him in some ways. She loved India, for the right reasons as I think. She loved the people. She was a very good Christian. I got my religion, certainly, mostly from her. She loved to talk about the ordinary people in India, although she wasn't there all that long. I suppose, looking back (she died when she was in her early fifties), India was part of her life as it was for all those thousands of people who were in the Indian Civil Service or the Navy or the Army. Even my grandfather is buried in India.

I can remember a strange little incident, which I suppose is revealing. When I was about twelve or thirteen and my father was home and we had our own house in Hampstead Garden Suburb or just near it, one evening around Christmas – the night was quite cold and dark – the bell rang and I went to the door and I saw an old Indian looking in through the glass pane. I opened the door and my father then came out and he said – not roughly, because he wasn't that kind of a person – 'No, there's nothing here for you.' I remember that incident to this day. It seemed to me a terrible thing, not only because he was black but because he was poor, and I couldn't believe that at Christmas time you could turn anybody away. And the fact that this incident has stayed in my memory so long shows that it must have meant something important to me, I suppose.

At school
(centre)

Otherwise it was a totally uneventful childhood. I then went to my public school, which was Lancing, a church school and a very typical English public school, except that I think it had moved quite a long way beyond the normal because relationships with the staff were particularly easy. There was no feeling that one was being kept down and we were allowed a great deal of freedom for those days. It was a marvellous place on the South Downs, and you had all the room in the world to move around in. It didn't put enormous emphasis on games which I was never much good at. I quite enjoyed playing rugger (although it was a soccer school) as it was easier, and if you're not any good at it soccer is rather a boring game; and I ran a bit.

Lancing, I think, was a place that allowed me to grow very much to be what I wanted to be. Because it was a church school, religion was very dominant. The chapel there is one of the finest modern Gothic buildings in England, and the fourth highest, and dominated the whole school. We used to have to go to chapel twice a day, and three times on Sundays. But again, in those days there wasn't any sense that this was peculiar: it was just something you accepted as part of the system and you went along with it. And enjoyed it, in fact. I enjoyed the music. Peter Pears, the singer, who was a bit older than me, was also at the school. He was an alto in the choir. There was a high standard of music.

Then I became interested in writing and I became the editor of the school magazine and I contributed to another literary magazine. I don't think I was in any way exceptional as a writer but it gave me a kind of fulfilment.

During those years the school had what was called a 'mission' down in Camberwell, which in those days was one of the very poorest slum areas in London. I used to go there with one or two friends, as we were invited to do, to stay down there and see how the other half lived you might say. It certainly had an impact on me because the kids were barefoot and obviously lots of them had rickets and were malnourished. So it was quite an eye-opener for somebody who had been brought up in Hampstead, and it certainly did something to turn my mind to the social divide in this country.

I can remember a general election, in the 1920s. One of the candidates was a man called Shapurji Saklatvala who was an Indian and a Communist. We held a school election at the same time – there was great political activity although it was all terribly immature.

It wasn't really until I got to Oxford in 1931 that I became politicised. I was at Oxford from 1931 to 1934 at Christ Church, which is a fairly wealthy college – not that I had all that much money. It was by that time clear that I ought to be ordained into the ministry of the church and it was the time when unemployment was enormously high. The hunger marchers, men from Jarrow, from South Wales, from the coalfields, from the docklands, marched to Westminster. Not in a militant way: they were just desperate for food. I saw them as they came through Oxford. They had to sleep in town halls, wherever they could get accommodation. And their plea was just to have a reasonable standard of living. You may remember that the settlement of the General Strike in 1926 was the most extraordinary and iniquitous ever because the miners were left with less pay than they had before it started.

So I was there at that time and it was a time of considerable political ferment. There was the great debate in the Oxford Union that 'This house will in no circumstances fight for king or country' which was won. It caused a tremendous upheaval. People said it was disgusting and disgraceful, and Winston Churchill's son came and tore the minute out of the minute book.

That was my first real taste of confrontation with a system which I regarded as unjust and this led me into Christian socialism. Many of my contemporaries had the same feeling.

During his years at Christchurch College, Oxford

I found myself involved in a very interesting summer school: it was called the Anglo Catholic Summer School and the subject was 'Marxism and Christianity'. We had some very distinguished speakers and I can remember them although many spoke in foreign tongues. Nicholas Berdyayev was a Russian Orthodox ex-Marxist and Julius Hecker came over from Moscow specially to address us and I believe T.S Eliot was there. It was quite high powered.

I think that got across for me, in a kind of academic perspective, what things were all about in Britain at that time. It was encouraging, really that that kind of issue was so much at the top of the agenda in Oxford in my day.

I can say that my real commitment to Christian socialism came eventually in action rather than in conferences. And of course, it didn't really flower until I got to South Africa itself. But before that, I was drawn very strongly to a religious order in the Anglican church called the Community of the Resurrection at Mirfield in Yorkshire, which was founded by a very remarkable Anglican bishop, Charles Gore (who is still commemorated by an annual lecture in Westminster Abbey) and who declared himself a Christian socialist and remained one. The community he founded always had that element in it. I, of course, didn't go there immediately to try my vocation but I went to visit it, and I was much impressed by the feeling of the community: the way the brethren were very aware of the world. It was not a reclusive community, it was an active missionary order. In its early days it was regarded by the Church of England as very left wing indeed because we invited Keir Hardie – one of the leaders of the Labour Party – to come and address a great mass meeting in the quarry at Mirfield. And always, even in my day, when general elections came up, the brethren were quite free to go and talk on Labour Party platforms, or wherever else they wanted to go.

So that socialist element was there. And it was very, very congenial to me. I can't say that then I knew terribly much about it in practice; nevertheless, that was my background from then on. I am still a member of the Community, it's still basically my home, and I hope to die there one of these days.

However I came down from Oxford and I had a few months to fill in before going for my theological training. My aunt who had brought me up, left me £500, quite a lot for those days, and I went off on a tramp steamer, first of all to what was then called Ceylon (now Sri Lanka), and then on a major trip through India to see the places where my father had lived and worked. In the course of it I went across to Burma and up the Irawaddy and right up to the Chinese frontier. At that time Ceylon, of course, was still part of the Raj. In the church it was very highly multiracial: every community of Sinhalese and Tamil and Burgher (as the white settlers were called) worshipped together. It was a very great experience of inter-ethnic worship. It certainly impressed me very much. I think it was almost a unique church in those days.

Then, having done that grand tour, I came back. In the Church of England part of your training is to go as a curate – it's called your 'title' and you do two or three years in a parish before you do anything else. Some clergy of course decide they want to be chaplain to a university but they're all

supposed to do a stint in a parish. Luckily for me – and again, this was through the Community because two of our members had worked in that parish – I was sent to St Mark's, Swindon. Swindon in those days was the real working headquarters of the Great Western Railway. All the people who belonged to the parish where I was a junior curate (there were seven of us) were employed by the Great Western Railway: they got up when the hooter blew; they knocked off when the hooter blew; and they went for their holidays two weeks at a time when they were told to. It was a marvellous working-class parish.

These experiences in Swindon didn't do anything to undermine my interest and concern in socialism. My time there ended early in 1939 and I knew then that I must go to Mirfield to the Community of the Resurrection and test my vocation – to see whether they would have me, and whether I would have them. That is what is called a 'novitiate'. I landed up there in about February or March 1939 - and of course within six months war was declared. So I was in a community that was cut off from its missionary work in Southern Africa, which was very considerable: we'd started educational work in what was then Rhodesia (now Zimbabwe) at the end of the last century. We were responsible in South Africa for the Anglican Church's work in primary and secondary education; and in Rhodesia we had a big secondary school and a teacher training college. So there was plenty of scope.

Although I didn't get to South Africa for four years, there were a lot of the brethren in the Community who had been out there. I couldn't get out there because we weren't allowed to (it was very difficult to get a passage), and they couldn't get home. Nevertheless, the South African background was very real, and when I took my vows after two and a half years – the vows of poverty, chastity and obedience, the traditional vows – I knew the chances were that when the time came I would be sent to South Africa, because all the younger brethren were asked to go there to get experience.

SOUTH AFRICA

I can remember very well the day that I left for South Africa. The war was still on. I had to sail in convoy from Liverpool and I can remember throwing my gas mask over the side when I got on to that boat – and of course I never saw the war again because South Africa was never hit in the same way by the war as Britain was. It was a remarkable thing to sail into Cape Town and see all the lights on and to go to a club and have a most marvellous meal.

Anyhow, my beginnings in South Africa were extraordinary really. I was pretty young – just thirty – for the job I was asked to do. The new Superior who had done the job before me sent me to Sophiatown, a black residential area in Johannesburg. It was separated by a few miles from what is today Soweto, the largest black township in South Africa. Sophiatown was much closer into the centre of the city.

I didn't know when I first arrived there how I was going to cope with it at all because I had this vast parish to look after with about seven churches and a large number of schools, including the largest primary school in South Africa, St Cyprian's. I can remember on the day I arrived there, the doors of the church opened and about two thousand kids poured out. And I thought, 'How the heck am I going to get to know any of them?' There were so many, of all different ages. For the first year or two I just had to find my feet. I had to run the place and I had to report to the bishop. I obviously knew very little.

Sophiatown

It was Sophiatown and Soweto that matured me, because I *felt* apartheid, as it affected the people I was looking after (particularly the young and the old), when I saw every day of my life what apartheid did to them. In those days particularly, it was the housing conditions, the pass laws and all that went with them – the segregated society which had been there for generations.

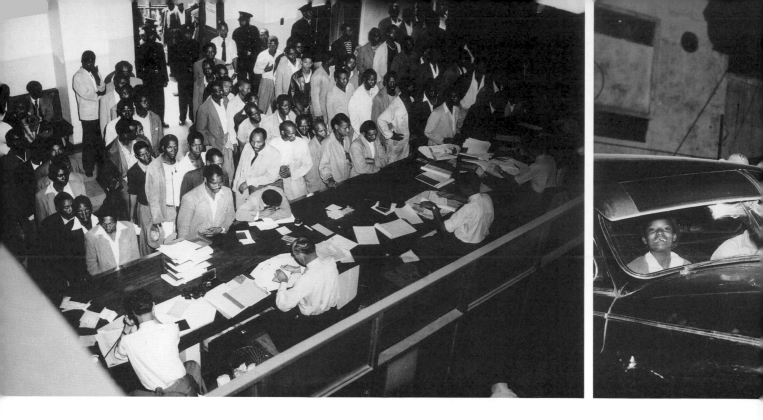

Pass Office (above)
Pass searches (above centre and above right)
Anti-pass demonstration broken up by police
(right)

I soon discovered that Sophiatown was a most vital place to live in, it was alive in a

special way – because it was very crowded –
but the people were a real community

Dr Xuma, R V Selope Thema, Professor Z K Mathews (5th from left),
Paul Mosaka, Albert Luthuli and Dr J S Moroka

At that time there were some very notable African leaders living in or around Sophiatown: for instance, the President of the African National Congress (ANC), Dr Xuma, lived just up the road from me, I knew him very well, and Selope Thema, who had been a member of the first Native Representative Council, and by this time was a kind of elder statesman. The presence of many such political leaders meant that we were automatically politicised.

Protest

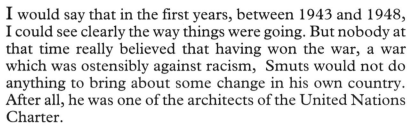

I would say that in the first years, between 1943 and 1948, I could see clearly the way things were going. But nobody at that time really believed that having won the war, a war which was ostensibly against racism, Smuts would not do anything to bring about some change in his own country. After all, he was one of the architects of the United Nations Charter.

THE VANDAL

And so there was a great feeling of hope in the air. I want to convey this because immediately after the war there were movements in the white community like the Torch Commando* (which I remember blessing when it left on its journey to Cape Town from the City Hall steps).

* The Torch Commando were World War II veterans opposed to the Nationalist government's attacks on the constitution, in particular on the limited voting rights still held by some black South Africans. They took their name from the torchlit processions of protest they organised.

All that, of course, came to an end in 1948 in the general election of that year when the National Party came to power and when Smuts himself not only lost the election as leader of his party, but lost his own seat. He never got back into the mainstream of politics again. I can remember that. I was ill with flu and I listened to the radio and I heard every result coming through with this extraordinary reversal. Smuts thought that because the war had been won, he would certainly get back into power. They were totally complacent, the so-called United Party.

First National Party Cabinet

So that was a crucial moment. And it was then that almost all the major legislation which today is structured apartheid, was passed. And yet from 1948 to 1956, when I left South Africa, it was still possible to hold massive protest meetings. We began, of course, in Sophiatown itself. I can remember meetings in what was then the Odin cinema. It was in those days a very posh cinema for Sophiatown, and a very good meeting place. It was the one place that I can remember where Nelson Mandela and I were on the same platform. It was a very crucial meeting because the police were ringing the building – there were thousands of people inside and thousands of people outside – and we really thought there would be bloodshed. We had to calm the people down. I've got a photograph of myself with one of the Asian leaders – with the police intervening.

Similar political events took place in Freedom Square in Sophiatown.

Other protests were held in Johannesburg by the white community, protesting against the major legislation of that time, like the Group Areas Act, the Bantu Education Act, the Prohibition of Mixed Marriages Act, and the Immorality Act. Such laws were never passed without protest, and I was certainly part of that protest.

STOP MALAN TERROR:

PROTEST NOW!

WITH SWART'S GESTAPO BILLS—

NO CONCENTRATION CAMPS

NO MARTIAL LAW

★STOP POLICE RAIDS   ●LIVING WAGES: LOWER PRICES

★FREE SPEECH & ASSEMBLY   ●DOWN WITH APARTHEID

There were very few white people in those days who lived in a black township. We were the only ones apart from a small Roman Catholic mission just up the road. Michael Scott, who was a great pioneer of rebellion, had been a chaplain at an orphanage not very far from where I lived, and I worked with him. At that time, too, the great squatter movement broke out in Orlando when thousands and thousands of homeless people built shacks on the edge of what was then called Orlando and Meadowlands, and which today is part of Soweto.

Those were years of intense commitment, leading up to the great day of the Congress of the People at Kliptown, just outside Johannesburg.

FREEDOM
r Day
to Kliptown
SUNDAY JUNE 24
at 9:30

FREEDOM
Come to Kliptown
SUNDAY JUNE 24
at 9:30

Also it was a meeting with a vital function. It had to pass the Freedom Charter clause by clause.

This was a great historic moment.

When people talk about the ANC as a 'terrorist' organisation, they haven't any understanding of its history, which goes back to 1912. When the Native Land Act was passed in 1913 Sol Plaatje and other leaders decided that they must make their protest at Westminster. A later delegation in fact was able to see the Prime Minister, Lloyd George, and make their protest.

(from l to r) R V Selope Thema, Solomon Plaatje, J T Gumede, Rev H Ngcayiya, L T Mvabaza

Yusuf Dadoo

A J Luthuli

But I am sure Kliptown will always be a real landmark in African history. Everyone was there who could get there. Of course Chief Luthuli was supposed to be there – he was then the President of the ANC – but he wasn't allowed to be there as he was restricted and banned. Yusuf Dadoo of the Transvaal Indian Congress was unable to go for the same reasons. I suppose I was the only one of the Isitwalandwe★ award winners who was able to get there, because I was white and because I was a clergyman. At that time I think clergymen were regarded as harmless. But I have tried to alter that in the course of my life!

★ Isitwalandwe is the highest honour awarded by the African National Congress.

I had matured both in my socialism and in my commitment: I believed most strongly that fighting apartheid was a moral battle against something profoundly evil. It didn't come to me through academic reading or study. It came to me through seeing apartheid in its impact on the people who I had responsibility for as a priest. And the marvellous thing to me has always been that those kids that I looked after are still in the forefront. Desmond Tutu is one of them. He was thirteen when I first knew him. He had very bad tuberculosis and he was on his back for two years in hospital. I used to visit him every weekend and take him books.

Another of the great excitements of Sophiatown in the years that I was there was the opportunity to build up a real cultural concern because the people were starved of music. There was a marvellous man called Joseph Tarneck who ran the Johannesburg Symphony Orchestra and he brought his entire orchestra out to Sophiatown. He became a regular visitor and a very great friend. They used to come on a Saturday afternoon and play in the school playground. And then, when visiting artists came from abroad under contract to white entrepreneurs, I used always to invite them to come and play in the church. The first, I think, who ever did was Yehudi Menuhin. He came and gave a concert in our church, which was packed. The Amsterdam String Quartet, which was very high powered, came and played in our little nursery school to an evening gathering, and they told me afterwards they'd never played to a more musical audience. This inspired me a great deal.

When I was promoted in my Community to be Provincial (that is I had to look after *all* the houses in the Community), it meant leaving Sophiatown physically and living in a place called Rossetenville where our big secondary school, St Peter's, was. I never really left Sophiatown, though, because the Community was still there and I was able to go there whenever I wanted to.

Here was another challenge. That school was very special in many ways. Oliver Tambo was a schoolmaster at St Peter's when I first knew him. Ezekiel Mphahlele, the writer, was another schoolmaster. People like the author Peter Abrahams were old boys of the school. It was obvious that we had a nucleus of children, both boys and girls, who were the future.

Luthuli with Oliver Tambo

E Mphahlele

Quite accidentally I hit on a way of mobilising culture for that generation. There was an epidemic of flu and I went up to the dormitory and there was a small boy called Hugh Masekela, who was recovering. He wasn't very ill but I just said to him, 'What would you like to make you better quickly?' And he

immediately answered, 'A trumpet.' I couldn't go back on my promise so I went and got him his first trumpet. Then of course everybody in the school wanted an instrument. I spent about a year begging instruments. I hadn't got any money – I had to beg the money as well as the instruments. And gradually we built up a really first-class jazz band. Hugh Masekela was the trumpeter. He really taught himself: the only thing I did was to get a Salvation Army trumpeter to show him how to blow because he was making such a filthy noise I thought the neighbours would break us down! Jonas Gwangwa was the trombonist, and Churchill Jolobe was the drummer.

At the same time, there were also young boys and girls who were heavily politicised. I suppose I did quite a bit of the politicising – I hope I did, anyhow. Their names, of course, are not so familiar as Oliver Tambo's but there were quite a number of others who in time found themselves committed to the struggle.

Those St Peter's years led me to the important understanding that one way of mobilising world opinion against South Africa was to plead for a cultural boycott: to say to artists of every kind, 'If you come to South Africa you are in fact supporting apartheid because you will only be playing (as they were in those days) to white audiences. So don't come.' And I wrote an article in the *Observer* (I've still got a copy of it) which I called 'The Church Sleeps On', and attacked the church for not being active in a world sense, and particularly in Britain, in support of the struggle.

The Church Sleeps On

By FATHER TREVOR HUDDLESTON, C.R.

JOHANNESBURG

I tell you naught for your comfort,
Yea, naught for your desire,
Save that the sky grows darker yet
And the sea rises higher . . .
—G. K. Chesterton:
"Ballad of the White Horse"

THE question which poses itself to any intelligent Christian in South Africa to-day is two-fold. How is he to persuade his fellow-Whites that they are in deadly danger of betraying their faith by ignoring its implications? How is he to persuade his African brethren that Christianity is a living religion which stands for certain fundamental principles—amongst them love and justice? Or—to put the position in a slightly different form—has the twenty-fifth hour already struck, and has the Church lost the battle in this day and generation?

I have come to the conclusion that in fact there is no future for the missionary work of the Church in South Africa unless it recognises at once that it is caught up into a tragic situation which needs immediate and desperate remedies. And I can see no sign either that the Church does recognise this fact, or that it has any real desire to apply swift and remedial action.

Marks of Tyranny

The Department of Native Affairs has recently issued a circular which makes it clear that any Church daring through its representatives to criticise Dr. Verwoerd, the Minister of Native Affairs, lays itself open to the closure of its missionary work in locations at three months' notice. I am now more convinced than ever that the State in South Africa has already become a tyranny—and that in consequence Christians with a conscience should be prepared to resist its laws and take the consequences. I should like to try to justify this statement with certain simple facts.

The basic conception of government which affects all legislation in the Union to-day is *not Apartheid*—though that is its corollary—but White supremacy. This is stated and admitted freely not only by the Government but by the Opposition—though in the latter case it is sometimes described rather differently. It is because the vast majority of the European population accept this concept as necessarily right that they are fully prepared to remain supine when it is implemented in act.

As I write, I have just had the news that one of my African friends, a devout Christian, has been banned and his movements proscribed for two years. This kind of procedure has now been taken against virtually all African and non-European leaders of any standing in South Africa, including a great many trade unionists. Yet, White South Africa remains silent, either approving wholeheartedly such totalitarian

methods or tacitly accepting them as part of a pattern of life which has become familiar.

And—here is the point—White South Africa is predominantly Christian. The missions are still prepared to negotiate with the Government—for instance, in the matter of native education; they are still prepared to believe (or are they?) that some good can come out of this great evil.

Clinging to Privilege

White Christians have voted the Government into power and are prepared to vote it into power again if this means that their position of privilege remains inviolate: if they can keep their native servant and their American motor-car: if they can hear the magic word "baas" wherever they may go.

Can it be that they have ever really read St. John's gospel describing the washing of the Disciples' feet by their Master? Can it be that they have ever heard His challenge to the complacent and self-satisfied: "If I, then, your Lord and Master, have washed your feet, ye also ought to wash one another's feet"?

The Church sleeps on. It sleeps on while 60,000 people are moved from their homes in the interests of a fantastic racial theory: it sleeps on while plans are made (and implemented) to transform the education of Africans into a thing called "Native Education"—which will erect a permanent barrier against Western culture reaching the African at all: it sleeps on while a dictatorship is swiftly being created over all Native Affairs in the Union, so that speech and movement and association are no longer free.

The Church sleeps on—though it occasionally talks in its sleep and expects (or does it?) the Government to listen.

What New Goal?

And so the day draws rapidly nearer when the African Christian will be unable any longer to accept the authority of that Church: when its authority will be so blurred, so formless, so entangled in his mind with the authority of the State, as to be an intolerable burden. *And he will cast it off.*

What authority he will then accept is anybody's guess: it doesn't much matter whether the Communist or the Nationalist ideal will be his goal. It will not be the Christian ideal. And to those of us who are in the midst of the struggle this thought is unbearable: it is a burden so heavy upon the heart that it cannot be borne indefinitely.

For here all is being broken by it—friendship, society, life itself. In God's name, cannot the Church bestir itself all over the world and *act*? Cannot Christians everywhere show their distress in practical ways by so

isolating South Africa from contact with all civilised communities that she realises her position and feels some pain in it?

I am pleading for a cultural boycott of South Africa. I am asking that all those who believe racialism to be sinful or wrong should refuse to encourage it by accepting any engagements to act, to perform as a musical artist or as a ballet dancer—in short, to engage in any contracts which would provide entertainment for only one section of the community. True, this will only be a demonstration. But I believe it will be quite an effective one. At least it will give White South Africans an opportunity of tasting the medicine they so freely give to their Black fellow-citizens — the medicine of deprivation and frustration. And at least it will be better—considerably better—than sleeping.

WORDS IN T

By IVOR

HAVING first opened a parcel containing a book called "The Complete Plain Word," by Sir Ernest Gowers, I next slit an envelope to find a kindly invitation to a cinema to see a new picture called "The Egyptian." Therein I am promised the products of CinemaScope, Stereophonic Sound, and the Anamorphic Lens, the last being described as Revolutionary. (Is it really safe to use that adjective as a form of praise in the United States?) It seemed to me only fair that Sir Ernest, whose admirable counsels on words and their usage are printed by the Civil Service (Stationery Office) for Civil Servants, should end by observing that officialese is not the only offender against short and simple terms.

We are forcefully acquainted, whenever we turn to learned works, with the horrors of Criticese, Psychologese, Medicese, Theologese and the rest. Pundits are as eager as urchins to show off their toys: they will ride a new polysyllable as gleefully as the small boy will project himself on the birthday "scooter" or roller-skates. But might not the simple folk who go to their Palaseum for thrills, laughter, and romance be let off the Stereophonic and the Anamorphic?

Moving Shapes

And what is this Anamorphosity? Moving shapes upward and onwards, I supposed, drawing on the musty deposits of a faraway classical education. But certainty had to be sought. My "Shorter Oxford English Dictionary on Historical Principles" (two vols.) told me that

Removals

I came back to Sophiatown at a particularly critical time when the government was determined to remove all 'black spots' (as they called them) from white areas and they picked on my parish. This was a population of something like 60 – 70,000 people. As soon as their plan (known as the Western Areas Removal Scheme) was promulgated, we knew we had to take action and we formed a protest group.

It was at that time that the people I'd known best to be involved in the struggle really came into their own. Nelson Mandela, needless to say, was one of them on the African side. But I also got to know Ruth First pretty well – she was a frequent visitor; so was Hilda Bernstein whom I knew exceedingly well – Violet Weinberg and Helen Joseph. They were all visitors to my office in Rossetenville and Sophiatown. And I think the Western Areas Removal Scheme did something else: it was the first time that the media from Britain sent their top correspondents to cover what was happening. So we had all the major 'heavies'. We had people like Cyril Dunne from the *Observer*, Rene McColl from the *Daily Mail* – everyone in fact who was in that line of business, whatever the political party their paper represented, was there. So we got an enormous amount of media coverage in Britain for the Removal Scheme.

Nelson Mandela and Ruth First

olet Weinberg (centre)   **Hilda Bernstein**   **Helen Joseph (centre)**

Advance

Registered at the General Post Office as a Newspaper

ADVANCE, THURSDAY, JUNE 18, 1953

PRICE 3d.

75,000 AFRICANS TO BE DUMPED ON BARE VELD

"COME NOW GIRLS PLAYTIME'S OVER"

The Nationalists in the Cape Provincial Council objected strongly to school [...] ing Malan at the cinema. Our cartoonist says this is probably what the children wou[ld ...] him.

Inhuman Plan For Western Areas

JOHANNESBURG.

THE 75,000 INHABITANTS OF THE WESTERN AREAS OF JOHANNESBURG THREATENED WITH REMOVAL TO MEADOWLANDS WILL DEFINITELY NOT BE PROVIDED WITH ALTERNATIVE ACCOMMODATION. THEY ARE TO BE GIVEN DR. VERWOERD'S "SITE AND SERVICE SCHEME" ONLY.

THIS WAS TOLD TO ADVANCE LAST WEEK BY MR. C. W. PRINSLOO, CHIEF INFORMATION OFFICER OF THE GOVERNMENT'S NATIVE AFFAIRS DEPARTMENT. BASIC SERVICES ONLY WOULD BE PROVIDED, WITH WATER AS FIRST PRIORITY AND SANITATION SECOND.

The news has heightened the already intense anger and resentment of the people, who will give an organised expression of their protest at a big conference planned to take place at the Odin Cinema, Sophiatown, on Sunday, June 28.

Mr. Prinsloo explained the scheme as follows:

The economically well-to-do in the Western Areas would be compensated for the loss of their homes in the Western Areas and with the funds they were paid out would be able to erect a new home in the Meadowlands area. They could submit plans for their houses and then erect them. The rest—Mr. Prinsloo referred to about 85 per cent—would probably need financial assistance, and loans for amounts like £50, £100 or £200 would be made available to help these people erect structures on their stands in Meadowlands.

Mr. Prinsloo said all services would be full-planned. Meadowlands he said, would not be like Moroka and Jabavu because the latter were "emergency camps under wartime conditions". Only absent from the Minister's Site and Service Scheme from the outset would be high standard housing. But the services would be provided.

"FIRMLY PLANNED"

Mr. Prinsloo said the removal would be "firmly planned both ways". It would not be "an unorganised stampede".

[...] about the provision of [...] the new Meadowlands [...] they would be "pro[...] dinary way by the [...] cerned".

[...] port (the Orlando [...] y overcrowded) Mr. [...] e Minister had approved a committee which was [...] Of the 2s. 6d. hous[...] by all employers, [...] unt was earmarked [...] rvices. It was estimated [...] Pretoria Services [...] g in £135,000 a year [...] t would be four or [...] amount in Johannes

Asked what the Government would do if the people of the Western Areas refused to move, Mr. Prinsloo said: "Is it likely?" He then added "It has not yet happened that they've refused. The Minister will meet difficulties as they come".

CALL FOR OPPOSITION

Father Trevor Huddleston last week urged, in an interview with Advance, that every single European organisation, including the churches, should insist that the Johannesburg City Council make clear

(Continued on page 5)

MORE RAIDS ON O[...] OFFICES

Police Look for Treason

JOHANNESBURG

MEMBERS of the political branch of the police again swooped on the offices of the Transvaal African and Indian Congresses [...] week armed with warrants empowering them to find [...] offences of treason, sedition or under the Suppression [...] Act, the Riotous Assemblies Act or the Crim[...] Act.

The raids took some hours, the detectives scrutinising files, all contents of drawers and cupboards and, as their warrant authorised them, searching for documents relating to the African National Congress, the South African Indian Congress, the Franchise Action Council, the Joint Planning Council, the National Action Committee, the Transvaal Indian Youth Congress, the Natal Indian Congress, the Cape Provincial Indian A[...] and the Springbok Legi[...]

Congress [...] for as lon[...] after a w[...] of the off[...] Congress[...] ceeding[...]

At [...] were [...] copy[...] thi[...]

That went on right through 1955 when the people were removed from their homes and their homes were bulldozed out of existence. They were dumped on a bit of open veld in Meadowlands on the edge of Soweto, and there was nothing that could be done because the force used to remove them was very massive. But don't forget, *that* removal was just part of the population removal which has been going on ever since. Up till now, over 3,500,000 people have been uprooted and moved.

So it was a very critical historical moment and I am thankful to have been there on the first day that it happened. I remember going out there early in the morning – the lorries were all lined up . . .

80

. . . and started bulldozing them straight away.

This was the end of Sophiatown.

It wasn't the end of the community in Sophiatown because that moved over in the end, basically, to Soweto. And they went with their political commitment. I knew very many Soweto people like Walter Sisulu and Albertina Sisulu: they were part of my parish. And all these people came into greater prominence because here was a focal point, something which everybody recognised as *the* hard cutting edge of apartheid – as it has proved to be. I would say that Removals and the Bantu Education Act were the two major issues.

Walter Sisulu, Ruth First and Albertina Sisulu

I did write about this very clearly at the time, and I tried to arouse world opinion on this issue because it seemed obvious to me that Verwoerd and 'grand apartheid' would take over and destroy so many people.

Even so, I knew – and I'm not saying this with hindsight – that we had such a quality of leadership in the African community, really great people, as the Robben Island prisoners have shown; as Oliver Tambo has shown, that we would be bound to win.

BRITISH WEEKLY

APRIL 5 1956   Volume CXXXVII   No. 3621

Registered at the General
Post Office as a Newspaper

Editor :
Shaun Herron
Address : 11 Buckingham Street,
Adelphi, London, W.C.2
Telephone : Trafalgar 2471-2
Price Fourpence

Postage on this Issue: At Home 1½d.—Abroad
1d. (if marked Printed Matter, Reduced Rate).

Trevor Huddleston

This Man's Cause Called for Our Support

Where were we and who stood between Huddleston and ourselves?

By SHAUN HERRON

I REMEMBER during the debate in our churches in Britain on the Bantu Education Act, a well-known churchman who invited or it said to me:—

"The trouble about Huddleston is that he wants to do something quick and dramatic. We on the other hand think this matter can only be dealt with at the painfully detailed level of everyday life."

I have always thought this a revealing and a silly thing to say. It reveals, for one thing, how little the man in question knew about detailed and everyday Christian witness in a world where the wordiness of the ecclesiastical smoothie is not enough.

There is nothing quick and dramatic about finding a dozen African families with the roofs torn off their houses by Order, and going to the Courts to plead for them, about rising, trembling with fear, and being threatened by the magistrate.

There is nothing quick and dramatic about bathing the babies of several hundred black mothers who are living under sacking in the open because thugs have driven them from their homes and the white authorities refuse to protect them.

The man who has found it so easy publicly and privately to scorn and deplore the life and witness of Trevor Huddleston would not be found doing any of these things. They are not dramatic but they demand more from a man than a notoriously fluid vocabulary and a notoriously smooth tongue. And of course, they are so practical as to be almost vulgar.

The Calling

Huddleston will never find a place in those circles where church-illy important people talk and talk and talk about the complexity of situations about which they should be doing something and are in fact merely devising plausible and elaborate evasions of any relevant action.

But he has found his place in Christian history as prophet, priest and saint. He has done more; his work will in time be gathered to the credit of the churches which spurned him, in more than one case maligned him, and in every case where profoundly disturbed by him:

disturbed as only a bad conscience can be disturbed. [Only S.P.G. has supported him with substantial funds.]

I want to ask you, please, to read Huddleston's book **Naught For Your Comfort** (Collins, 12s. 6d.). I hope young men and women will sacrifice pleasures to buy it. I hope laymen and women will give it to their ministers especially their young ministers, so that they may not forget the calling wherewith they were called, even if their congregations would prefer them to.

He takes his title from Chesterton's **Ballad of the White Horse.**

**I tell you naught for your comfort,
Yea, naught for your desire,
Save that the sky grows darker yet
And the sea rises higher.**

His book is a story of tragedy, the tragedy of the church. The case so complacently presented to our churches in this country during that debate has since those days been shot to pieces by events. I have waited before printing this article about Huddleston and his book, to see what the secular journals said about it? Is it worth noting in Christian circles that the common people heard him gladly? Huddleston is welcome among men; the case put up by the churches against him and against action was received with contempt: is there a reason for this?

Obedience

It is too easy to dig around among the mental health specialists to find an answer. Say if you like, that it is sinful man's nostalgic tribute to Goodness. Then what does sinful man's contempt for the Churches' failure in Africa mean—or does our perpetual religious dishonesty turn from answers we do not want?

Here in this book, Christian people are confronted by the heart and mind of a man who takes Christ seriously. He is a fallible man: he judges Calvinism by the Dutch Reformed Church's perversion of it. Those who care about the main issue do not care whether Huddleston is "Catholic" or "Calvinist," they care only that he took His yoke upon him, and, in doing so, went to the heart of the matter.

There are situations in history when the church cannot claim any

meaningful measure of obedience to her Lord unless she confronts a situation without compromise and with the cry: **We must obey God** rather than men. The minority Confessing church in Germany did it over the Aryan clause prohibiting Jews from worshipping with "Aryans."

The South African Churches faced the same challenge once the Nationalists declared themselves and began making laws that violated the whole purpose of Christian mission history in Africa and confronted the churches also with a choice between a denial of the Gospel or a denial of the law. But the Confessing church in South Africa consisted of Huddleston, Reeves, Jack Grant, and the Roman Church.

Timid Policy

A former President of the South African Methodist Conference declared recently in an interview published in a religious paper in this country that all the South African churches are fighting **apartheid.** The best comment that can be made on such a claim is this: the African paper **Drum**, recently sent a reporter and a photographer on an attempt to enter and remain in White churches in Johannesburg. They were thrown out of every one they tried to enter. One of the men was black. Why did they send a photographer? To record the Churches struggle against **apartheid**, of course. Maybe Africans are cynical about Christian Churches?

The Christian Council of South Africa, after much hesitation on the part of some of its members, asked the Minister of Native Affairs for an interview in connexion with his vindictive closing of the Anglican school of Christ the King. He curtly refused to meet them.

The timid policy of the churches has been treated with contempt by the Nationalists. Almost every churchman in the Union claims that Huddleston's methods have failed because he has roused the hostility of the government. It is not a new view of Christian obedience that it is incumbent upon us only when it does not arouse hostility. **But as a matter of practical politics, how far has the timid subservience of the Churches got them?** And since when has "failure," to a Christian, been the measure of right and wrong action?

This kind of reasoning throws the gospel out of the Church—and then what is the church?

The whole tragic issue is summed up in the Archbishop of Canterbury's account of his visit to him, during which the Archbishop told Huddleston how wrong he was. "You are entirely wrong in the methods you are using to fight this situation . . . The Christian must never use force . . . must never use the weapons of his opponent."

'Symbolic'

This statement will astonish all who know that Dr. Fisher considers it right to use anything that will deter Communism. It will astonish all who wonder about the Christian responsibility in time of war, for the Archbishop was not previously known to be a pacifist. The Archbishop told Huddleston that Jesus turning the moneychangers out of the Temple was only "symbolic." Sometimes it justifies the use of force and sometimes it is "symbolic"? That is handy.

But what is "force"? Huddleston appealing to the rest of the world for a "spiritual boycott" of South Africa? Huddleston going to court with a group of Africans whose houses have been torn down and whose families have been thrown into the street? Huddleston asking police to leave a meeting being held on church premises? Huddleston begging for money to cover the naked, persecuted and exposed? Huddleston saying "**Thus saith the Lord . . .** "? Huddleston admitting that as he rose in Court, to plead for black parishioners, he trembled with fear?

Vindication

The Gospel itself is **force.** It is force that good men have tried to stifle and control in every generation. And in this generation we are adding daily to the tragedy of Christian disobedience. **The Church has been** wrong, every time her courage and faith, have been challenged. **The Gospel has been vindicated by** men like Huddleston and Reeves and Scott, in every generation.

At Evanston they resolved that where men stand out and feel it laid upon them to obey God rather than men, the church must support them.

And men returned from Evanston to this country—and to Africa—to busy themselves with this task of depriving Grant, Reeves, Huddleston and Scott of their support of the Church.

Calvary

Huddleston says:

"If I am mistaken, as well I may be, in the methods I have used: then I trust in the mercy of God for my forgiveness. For He, too, is a Person. And it is His Person that I have found in Africa, in the poverty of her homes, in the beauty and splendour of her children, in the patience and courtesy of her people. But above all, I have found Him where every Christian would expect to find Him: in the darkness, in the fear, in the blinding weariness of Calvary.

"And Calvary is but one step from the Empty Tomb."

"I wish," said a young African, of this son of the living God "I wish he was black." And when some of the White detractors in high places in our churches read his book, maybe they will be inclined to tell him how wrong were their private charges against him. If, that is, they are ever aware of the possibility that they can be wrong.

Huddleston bids farewell to Sophiatown following his recall to his religious community in England

When I was recalled from South Africa by my own Community, I thought at that time I'd never get back to Africa again. And in fact, I had a special job to do which is not always very easily understood outside church circles: I was made what they call 'guardian of novices' in my own religious community.

I had been away for over 13 years and I hadn't a clue about the generation of men who were seeking to try their vocation in a religious order. So I had to learn all that.

At the same time my book *Naught For Your Comfort* had just been published and I was called away again and again to address public meetings all over England. It was a very difficult thing to hold together: a job which really required me to be with about 20 young men I was training, and at the same time go off talking about South Africa. It was very painful having to talk about South Africa all the time. However, thank God, after a couple of years I was removed to London for a brief period and then, quite out of the blue, came the news that I'd been elected bishop of the diocese of Masasi in southern Tanzania. So I heaved a great sigh of relief to be able to leave England and to go back to Africa.

THIS IS BOYCOTT MONTH

NEW AGE

6, No. 21. Registered at the G.P.O. as a Newspaper

NORTHERN EDITION   Thursday, March 10, 1960   **6d.**

IN SOUTH AFRICA AND ABROAD, FREEDOM FIGHTERS LAUNCHED BOYCOTT CALLS THIS MONTH.

● In Britain the month of March has been set aside for an intensified boycott of South African goods in protest against apartheid.

● In South Africa the Congress movement has called for a complete boycott of all celebrations connected with the Union Festival.

Trevor Huddleston addressing the enormous crowd which gathered in Trafalgar Square, London, to launch the boycott of South African goods.

BRITISH RESPOND TO BOYCOTT CALL

Mass Opposition To Apartheid

From Tennyson Makiwane

LONDON.

DESPITE the attempts of the right-wing press to play down the boycott (and the Mosley fascists to break it up), enthusiasm for the boycott of South African goods is mounting.

Seldom has an issue like this been so prominently splashed in the British press, debated radio and television, and there is no doubt it has made its mark on the British public.

AFTER an impressive march of 1½ miles, thousands of people led by a brass band entered Trafalgar Square here on Sunday, February 28, to support the boycott of South African goods.

At the head of the marchers were Trevor Huddleston, who had to his gown the "Isithwalandwe" medal presented to him at the Congress of the People in South Africa in 1955; Labour leader Hugh Gaitskell and several M.P.s including Jeremy Thorpe of the Liberal Party.

Altogether 8,000 people crammed the square to listen to the speeches. The crowds cheered and raised a forest of hands when the resolution calling for the boycott was put to the meeting. Other resolutions included a message to the British Prime Minister calling on him and his family to boycott South African goods; and also one to the African National Congress and other organisations in South Africa expressing solidarity with them in the struggle against apartheid.

MOSLEY'S FASCISTS

Throughout the meeting 4 or 5 lorries belonging to the Mosley fascists circled the square displaying anti-boycott slogans and generally trying to provoke the crowd. Some Mosleyites carried banners reading "Britons Awake — Be Right, Buy White".

The march to Trafalgar Square started shortly before 2 o'clock. A

(Continued on page 8)

"DON'T TAKE PART IN FESTIVAL OF SLAVERY"

Says Congress

JOHANNESBURG.

"DO NOT TAKE PART IN THE OFFICIAL CELEBRATIONS—FOLLOW THE CONGRESS and FIGHT FOR FREEDOM," says the leaflet issued by the Congress movement on the Union Festival celebrations which opened last week with official 'Whites Only' parades in several parts of the Union.

The Government will stage games for school children, says the leaflet but "we demand an end to police oppression and freedom for all".

MOURN FOR THE LOSS OF FREEDOM

Don't Forget To Wear Something Black For The Duration Of The Festival —From Now Until May 31.

By Order of Congress.

The folder is illustrated with drawings of what 50 years of Union has brought:
● Pass laws,
● Ghettoes,
● Bantu Education,
● Hunger, Low wages.

It says: Fifty years ago in 1910 the European governments of the Cape, Natal, the Transvaal and the Orange Free State united to form one central government and the Union of South Africa.

Fifty years ago white supremacy was established by the Act of Union.

What are we to celebrate?
● We have been robbed of our rights to our land.
● We have been given colour bars, pass laws, raids and police rule.
● Our leaders have been banned and banished.
● Our women have been forced to carry the hated pass that brings prison, separation and suffering to all.
● Our children have become victims of Bantu Education, denied the right to proper learning, the universities closed to them.
● We may not live where we choose, work where we choose, move around freely like free men.
● Our cattle have been culled.
● Taxation has been increased and extended to our women to impoverish us.
● Bantu authorities and Bantustans have been imposed on us.
THE UNION FESTIVAL CELEBRATES 50 YEARS OF SLAVERY.
BOYCOTT THE OFFICIAL CELEBRATIONS.

50 YEARS OF UNION HAS BROUGHT THIS —

PASS LAWS

GHETTOES

BANTU "EDUCATION"

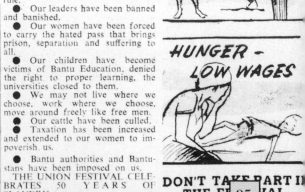

HUNGER - LOW WAGES

DON'T TAKE PART IN THE FESTIVAL CELEBRATIONS!

TANZANIA

Of course, the Africa I went back to was totally different from the great urban African townships of Johannesburg and the Reef. This was an entirely rural area. The people that I came to serve were peasant farmers. Ninety per cent of them were reliant on good weather for their crops: if they had a good year they could sell what they grew, they could raise their living standards a little; if it was a bad year, they had nothing. And quite often in that part of Tanzania the rains failed, the drought came, and it was a very, very difficult time for the whole community. Whole villages sometimes just had to get up and move because they hadn't got enough water.

So it was a very new experience and at the same time I was bishop for the first time. I had overall responsibility for a diocese the size of England. It was also a scattered diocese. We had only two major small towns – they were on the coast, the port town of Mtwara and the port town of Lindi. Otherwise all the parishes that I looked after were in little country villages scattered over that great area. It was a fascinating and marvellous experience to have to adapt to rural Africa. I had to learn from scratch the real meaning of rural life. I had been brought up in a town, after all, in England and I had worked in a town in Johannesburg. Now I was in a rural area.

In addition to that, I had to learn the language, Swahili, because without it I couldn't even talk to my own clergy. Swahili is a marvellous language but it took me at the age of 49, which I was then, about three years to become fluent in it. I think when you're that age it's much more difficult. When you're young, you have the opportunity of just moving around and listening. I got stuck into learning the grammar but then I invited children to come to my house so that I could practise my Swahili – I didn't mind making mistakes with kids and they enjoyed it. And, of course, they also spoke the purest kind of Swahili.

I had one enormous advantage in going to Tanzania because I had already met Julius Nyerere who was leader of the party which at the time of independence took over as the government. He was Chief Minister when I arrived in Tanzania but I had already met him in London. In fact he and I were on the platform at the launching of the Anti-Apartheid Movement so, as it were, we understood each other very well. In the years that I was there in Tanzania I had plenty of opportunities for meeting him and getting to know him better.

This was a great advantage because I was there, after all, at a crucial time. I arrived in 1960, a year before independence; I was there, therefore, in the last year of what you might call the colonial regime. So for a year I was there under the old administration, and this was very interesting because in Tanzania, unlike some other colonies, relationships with the administration, the British Colonial Service, were very good. I think it was because Tanzania is such a marvellous country that many of those who were sent to administer it fell in love with it and really enjoyed the people, as they should.

They are wonderful people, the Tanzanians, as they have proved over and over again in the struggle against apartheid by being a Front Line state which has just done everything to support liberation movements. In fact, during the time that I was in Tanzania, our border, of course, was the Mozambique border, and Frelimo, the liberation army, and Samora Machel were actually training in my diocese.

There were about 30,000 of them. I didn't know at the time that Machel was my next door neighbour because it was all top security. But I did meet Eduardo Mondlane, the founder of Frelimo who was later assassinated, more than once.

My concerns were really to get to understand what it would be like to live in a country which was discovering its own identity as a free, independent and sovereign state. This was very exciting. When I went to Masasi, we had the usual set-up: District Commissioner, Assistant District Commissioner, District Medical Officer, District Veterinary Officer, all of them white. After independence in 1961, they withdrew within a few months. They didn't withdraw altogether from Tanzania because quite a number stayed on in the capital, but not in the rural areas. This is the biggest criticism that I would make of the colonial administration: that it was an administration which did nothing, absolutely nothing, to prepare the people for independence and sovereignty. And so, when the British colonial civil servants withdrew (and I can say this with absolute accuracy), the only really educated person in the administrative headquarters in Masasi was an Asian filing clerk.

Think of the colossal job President Nyerere really had to face: to provide an administration for a country of that size. Tanzania is twice the size of France. They had to use all those people who could be found, in education, for example – school teachers – to build on until an effective administration could be built up.

NYERERE

FREEDOM AND UNITY | UHURU NA UMOJA

I was there also for the most important and significant political event, which was the very remarkable Arusha Declaration – Arusha is a large town in the north of Tanzania. Nyerere, who by then had become President, an Executive President, had worked for a long time on the principles of the Arusha Declaration. In fact, when he became, as he did at first, Prime Minister, he resigned and retired for a whole year from political life. He didn't know whether he'd be re-elected, he didn't know whether he would come to the very top again, but he was determined to think out the principles on which Tanzania should develop.

The Arusha Declaration was a very important milestone, not only for Tanzania but I think for the whole of Africa. Zambia, particularly, picked up on some of the elements in it. The two main elements, in Swahili, were 'ujamaa', which Julius Nyerere defined as African Socialism, and 'kujitegemea' which really means 'self reliance'. On those two principles he tried, and in many respects succeeded, to build the new country. I was there for that process.

It was fascinating, because I had been in confrontation with a white minority government all the time I was in Johannesburg, and in South Africa I had had to confront apartheid because of its evil impact on individual people. Now I was in a country with an African government, freely elected by the democratic process. We, the white community in Tanzania, were a very small minority, yet it was marvellous to be able to work one hundred per cent *with* the government because I believed fully in the principles on which it was based. And I say that as a Christian leader, too. My job really was to activate the Christian community as far as the Anglican church was concerned, to recognise that in those two principles of African Socialism and self reliance, they were actually able to build their country on sound lines.

Of course, there are many, many more things I could say about Tanzania because I learnt so much from the people there, and still do. I am President of the Britain – Tanzania Society and we've got a lot of rural projects in Tanzania still. So I am able to go there and see how things are developing. And I've been able to keep up my friendship with Julius Nyerere. It was wonderful to have had the opportunity of those eight years discovering what it meant for a new nation to find its identity.

Obviously there were problems, as every new country has problems. But I believe still that Tanzania has made a major contribution in the struggle for liberation in Southern Africa. At every point it has opened its doors to those who were leading the liberation struggle, whether they came from Mozambique or from what was Rhodesia or from any other neighbouring country seeking liberation. Tanzania was both a model and a friend, and it remained so because the African National Congress has strong educational bases in Tanzania, and no doubt it will play a very important role in the next decade or so.

ANC DEVELOPMENT CENTRE DAKAW

SOLOMON MAHLANGU

FREEDOM COLLEGE

A. N. C. (SA)

STEPNEY

111

Dan Jones '7

However, I knew that my job in Tanzania was to train African leadership in the church – that my job was to work myself out of a job, in fact – so that there would be an African bishop, an African education secretary for the diocese and so forth. And that time I expected would be about ten years. In fact it was only eight and I came back to England at the invitation of the then Bishop of London to be assistant bishop, or suffragan bishop as it is called, in the East End of London, in Stepney.

I can't tell you what the culture shock was like, coming out of a country like Tanzania with a peasant farming population in a very poor area of a very poor country, and coming back to the urban area of London which was always described as the most deprived area of London, the East End. My area of jurisdiction as a bishop was three boroughs, Tower Hamlets, Hackney and Islington, and today Hackney and Tower Hamlets are the most deprived boroughs in London. But I came back and I saw shops bursting with goods. I had kids who said they were going to get Christmas presents costing 70 quid, and so forth. And that was a year's wage – if it was a good year – in Masasi. I didn't know what had hit me! I couldn't believe that people could say they were poor. The children in Masasi never had more than one meal a day. The greatest treat I could give to kids was to go in the Land Rover with them down to the sea, stop on the way, and the meal that gave them most delight was just a plate of rice and some fish and the gravy the fish was cooked in. That was a treat. And every child would have to come to school, not on a full belly at all, but waiting until school was over to walk home, perhaps two or three miles, before they got their main meal. So you can see, deprivation means different things wherever you are.

I came to learn during the ten years I was in Stepney a great deal about deprivation. And I think deprivation in an *affluent* society is infinitely worse than poverty in a Third World society which has marvellous values of community, of sharing and all that goes with it.

Celebrating his 70th birthday with children at the Huddleston Centre, Stepney.

I came to Stepney at an interesting time. It was in 1968 and it was the time when the Pakistanis from East Pakistan (as it then was, today it is Bangladesh) were coming into that area which has always been a great immigrant area in Britain. If you read history at all, you know that those who were refugees from religious persecution or whatever kind of persecution it was, came up the Thames, landed in the poorest area in London, and got a foothold there simply because they were so poor. We have had waves of immigrants over the last three centuries, starting with the French Huguenots, who were refugees from religious persecution in France – remarkable people in their own right, but very poor when they landed in Stepney. They had to make their way, and they did it by setting up silk weaving. In my house in Commercial Road I had a mulberry tree which was planted by the Huguenots and there were plenty of them all over the East End of London.

I came just at the time when a very nasty and very sinister upsurge of racialism was taking place – 'Paki-bashing' it was called. At that time in 1968 the Pakistanis were desperate, because they were so poor and they were easily identified by their colour. They were identified in other ways too – by their religion, by their language – and they had to find a foothold. And don't forget, that part of London has always been a base for fascism and racism. It was Oswald Mosley in the 1930s who recognised this, when in fact the immigrant community, although it had been there a very long time, was the Jewish immigrant community which had fled the Tsarist persecutions in Russia and Poland. And Mosley thought that he could use his racism to best effect by attacking the Jews. There was a march he planned, and there was a great battle, still remembered in the East End very vividly, the 'Battle of Cable Street', which the police were unable to control and the fascists became the victims of it, because the Jews and the Irish combined to bash them. And that has never been forgotten.

CABLE St. STEPNEY.

But these poor Bangladeshis or Pakistanis came into that sort of situation. So in my first couple of years I was very heavily involved in protest meetings and leading delegations to the House of Commons, in doing the sort of thing I was able to do in my first years in Sophiatown before the present Nationalist government came to power in South Africa and imposed much more repressive laws.

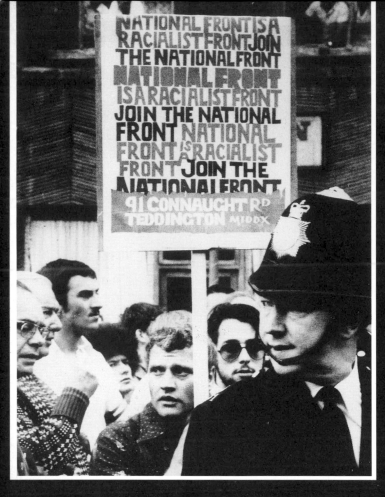

I am sad to say that that element of racism still persists, although the Bangladeshis have well established themselves and they are a very large community now.

So it was a challenging time to be there from that point of view. It was always very exciting for me to be in an area where the church was a small minority and where in fact we had to try and build up a community. In other parts, in Hackney and in Islington, the Caribbean community had settled in very large numbers. So it was a multiracial church, but not as multiracial as it ought to have been because I am afraid one of the ways in which the establishment of the Church of England operates is to make people who come from overseas, who are devout members of the Anglican communion, feel a kind of cold   shoulder at going into churches which are too 'respectable' or too Western in the wrong sense of that word.

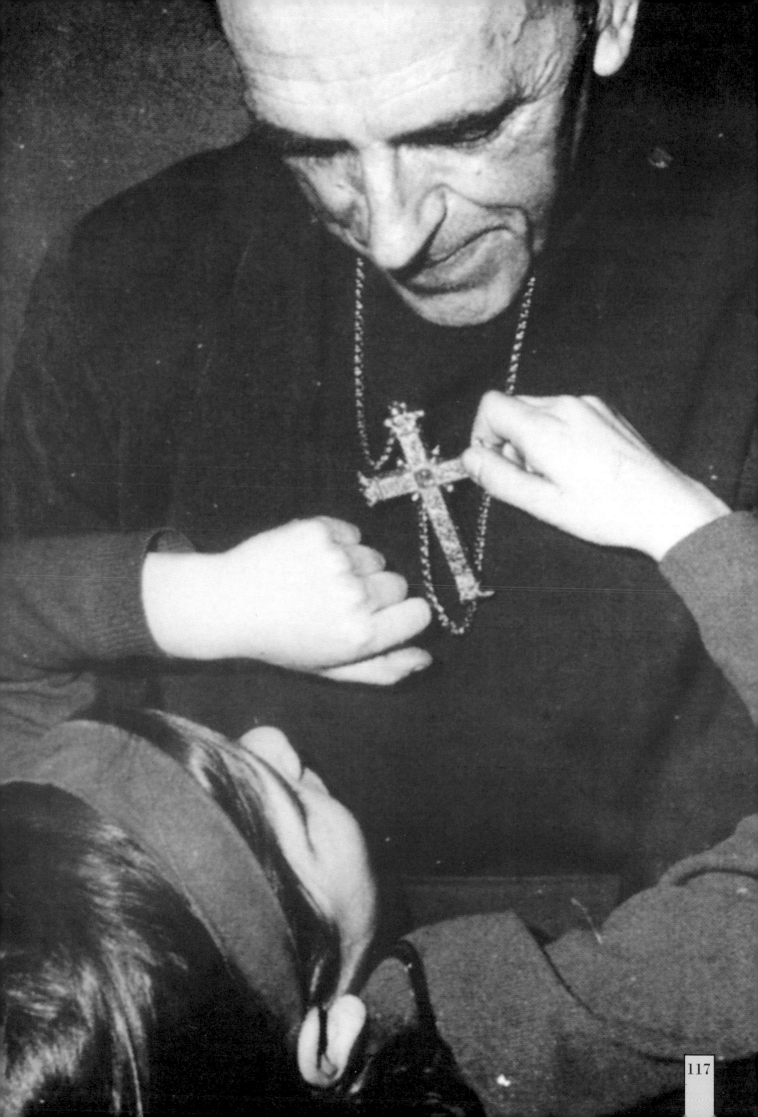

ATLANTIC

OCEAN

SAO TOME AND PRINCIPE
Sao Tomé

EQUATORIAL GUINEA

GABON
Libreville
Port-Gentil
Lambaréné
Mont Iboundji 1580
Franceville
Iguéla
Mouila
Tchibanga

CAMEROON

Ouesso
Mekambo
Mitzic
Fort-Rousset
Booué

Congo
Zaïre
Basankusu
Befale
Basoko

Mbandaka (Coquilhatville)
Bikoro
Ikela
Mossaka
Lac Mai-Ndombe
Kutu
Lokolama
Lomela

ZAIRE
Kindu
Bena-Dibele
Ilebo

Kisangani (Stanleyville)
STANLEY FALLS
Margherita Pk. 5109
Ubundi
Kasese

Kamp

Kigali
RWANDA
BURUNDI
Bukavu
Bujumbur

Lake Albert
Bunia

Kibangou
Dolisie
Brazzaville
Pointe-Noire
CABINDA (Angola)
Cabinda
Boma
Matadi
M'banza Congo
N'zeto
Ambriz
Negage

Bandundu
Kasai
Kinshasa (Léopoldville)
Kikwit
Popokabaka
Cuango
Feshi
Tshikapa
Kahemba
Sanza Pombo

Tshofa
Kongolo
Kalemie (Albertville)

MONTS MITUMBA
Ujiji
Lake Tangan

Kananga (Luluabourg)
Mbuji-Mayi (Bakwanga)
Chitato
Kaniama
Caungula
Camissombo
Kapanga
Kasongo

Manono

Lubudi
Kamina
Kawambwa
Lake Mweru
Kasenga

Luanda
Caxito
Dondo
Porto Amboim
Cela

ANGOLA
Malanje
Saurimo
Kasaji
Luau
Kolwezi
Likasi (Jadotville)
Lubumbashi (Elisabethville)
Kitwe
Mufulira
Ndola
Luanshya

Lobito
Serra Môco 2619
Kuito
Munhango
Luena
Solwezi

CABO DE SANTA MARIA

Huambo (Nova Lisboa)
Caconda

Luanguinga
Balovale
ZAMBIA
Kabwe (Broken Hill)

Lubango
Namibe
Kuvango
Menongue
Kassinga
Caiundo

Mussuma
Mankoya
Mumbwa
Mongo
Lusaka
Zambezi
Zumbo

N'Riquinha
Senanga
Choma
Chinhoy

Foz do Cunene
Cunene
Xangongo
Ondangua
Cuangar
Okavango
Cuangar
Shakawe
CAPRIVI STRIP

Livingstone
Lake Kariba
Harare

CAPE FRIO
OVAMBOLAND
Tsumeb
Okavango Swamp
Hwange
ZIMBABWE
Kwekwe

Sesfontein
NAMIBIA
Toteng
Gweru
Bulawayo
Gwanda

2606 Brandberg
Okahandja
Windhoek
(S. Afr. Admin.)
Ghanzi
Makgadikgadi Pans
Francistown
Shashi
Mwe

Walvisbaai
Walvis Bay (S. Afr.)

BOTSWANA
Serowe
Palapye
Messina
Louis Trichardt
Limpopo

Tropic of Capricorn

The United Nations declared an end to the mandate
of South Africa over Namibia in October, 1966.
Administration of the territory by South Africa
is not recognized by the United Nations.

Mariental
Gibeon

KALAHARI
DESERT
Kakia
Mochudi
Kanye
Gaborone
Zeerust

Pietersburg
Potgietersrus
Thabazimbi

Pretoria
Ma
Mai

Keetmanshoop
Aus

Koes
Kuruman
Vryburg

JOHANNESBURG
Springs
Klerksdorp
Vereeniging
Mbaban
SWAZI LAND

Askham
Welkom
Virginia
Kroonstad
Bethlehem

Bogenfels
Karasburg
Upington
Orange
Kimberley
Bloemfontein

Kroonstad
Ladysmith

Alexander Bay
Port Nolloth
Pofadder
Kenhardt
Injasuti 3408
Pieterm
burg

Springbok
SOUTH
Springfontein
De Aar
LESOTHO
Durb
Port She

Garies
AFRICA

Vanrhynsdorp
Clanwilliam
Lambert's Bay
Beaufort West
Murraysburg
Middelburg
Queenstown
Graaff-Reinet
TRANSKEI

Miller Oblated Stereographic Projection

Saldanha
GREAT KARROO
Laingsburg
Paarl
Cape Town
Swellendam
CAPE OF GOOD HOPE
CAPE AGULHAS
Mosselbaai
Uitenhage
Port Elizabeth
East London

Archbishop of the Indian Ocean

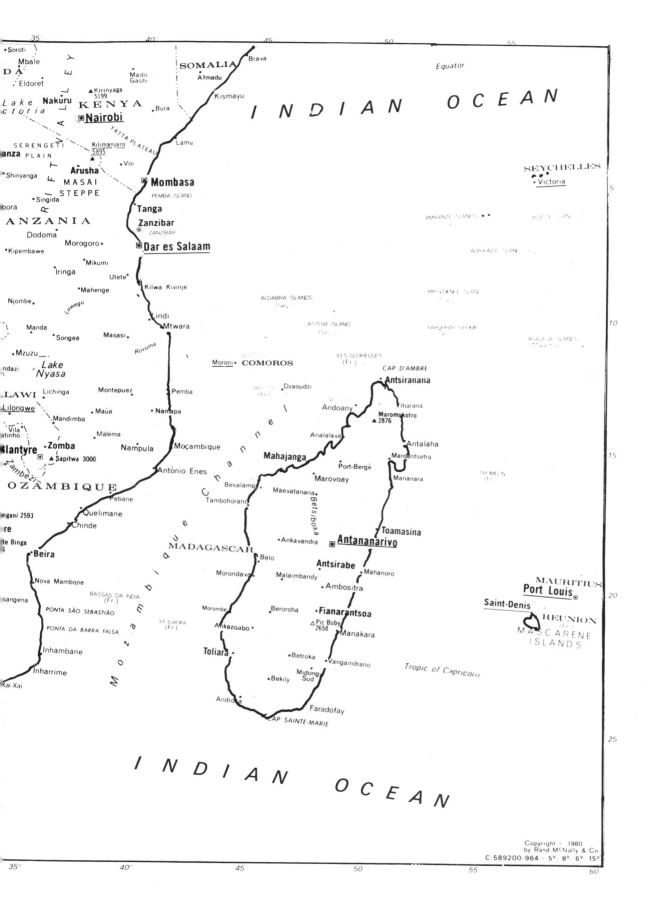

After ten years in Stepney I decided it was time for me to go as I was already 65. Quite unexpectedly, out of the blue, I received an invitation from the Diocese of Mauritius in the middle of the Indian Ocean to come and help them. The first Mauritian bishop died within six weeks of being made a bishop – he was quite young – and they didn't know where else to look, I suppose. They'd heard rumours that I might be available and of course for me this was a marvellous new chance, and so I set off for Mauritius. When I got

there they had to elect an Archbishop, so within a couple of weeks of being in Mauritius I was made an Archbishop and that meant I had to look after the Anglican church in the marvellous island of Madagascar and the islands of the Seychelles as well as in Mauritius. I had a pretty wide brief and I was called Archbishop of the Indian Ocean which caused a lot of ribald comment – because most of my parishioners were fish, I suppose they thought.

Mauritius is unique in that it was an uninhabited island with no aboriginals. The population came with colonialism and as they had no labour they got slave labour from India. Sugar was the basis of the economy. So the population, from Africa, Asia and Europe, is a microcosm of the world, with all the world religions – Hindus, Muslims and Buddhists and a minority of Christian churches, mainly Roman Catholic because of the French colonial influence. And so for me it opened up a completely new vista of what I would call inter-cultural, inter-faith relationships.

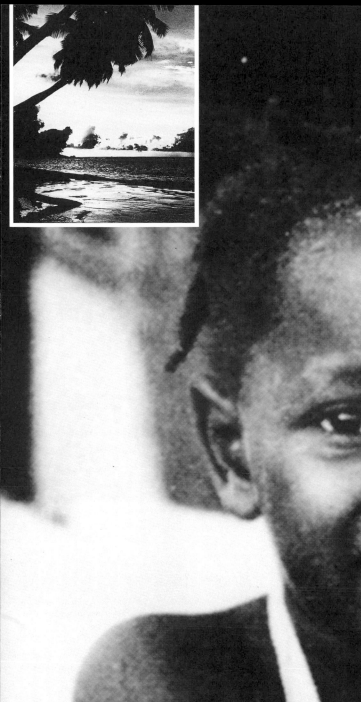

Madagascar is exciting in a different way because I suppose it is one of the least known countries in the world. It has enormous potential and is very beautiful and vast. I lived in Mauritius but I visited Madagascar quite frequently and moved around the country. I had three dioceses to look after there. It was while I was in the Seychelles that the strong, long arm of South Africa came into play because, towards the end of my time, the South Africans decided to try and overturn the government which was not in their favour, as it were. They were quite determined to do so and so they sent a mercenary force. Because of a very alert customs officer, a woman, who spotted the barrel of a gun sticking out of their luggage, they were caught and stopped in their tracks. It is a very interesting example of the policy of destabilisation and how it reaches right into the Indian Ocean – and still does, of course. Strategically it's very important to the major powers. You've got the two – on the one hand the Soviet Union with a vast navy in the Indian Ocean, and on the other hand the Western powers with their navies. Frequently, you would have war ships coming into Mauritius on courtesy calls.

I remember a garden party in the Governor General's house in Mauritius. In one corner of the garden was a bunch of Russian naval officers; in another corner there were the Chinese; in another corner there were the British and French. Of course, South Africa is an Indian Ocean state in the sense that it has a border on the Indian Ocean. The South Africans were very alert in trying to destabilise the Seychelles because it's got a very important international airport and harbour. So I didn't escape apartheid policies there either.

My time in the Indian Ocean was a wonderful experience. I came back to England completely convinced, from the religious side particularly, that what we'd got to do was to have dialogue with people of other faiths.

I launched a series of evenings in my own house – there was a vast veranda and dining room in the bishop's house there, it would seat 100 people. I chose the subject 'What is Man?'. I got a Christian, a Hindu, a Muslim, even a Marxist view, because I had a rather distinguished Marxist staying there at that time. And people came in great numbers because they'd never really had an opportunity to discuss these things. I was very glad to be there.

I was in Mauritius for five years. They went very quickly and I learned an awful lot there. And my greatest joy was my visits to Madagascar and to the islands. It was very rewarding in every way. When I went there I decided that I was not going to stay more than five years as I would be 70 by then. So I left and came back to London.

I went back to my Community up in Yorkshire at Mirfield but I found that impossible because I was spending all my time on the train to London commuting. I had become Chairman of the International Defence and Aid Fund and President of the Anti-Apartheid Movement and I didn't want to be a nominal president, stuck away up in Yorkshire. I wanted to take part in the activities and so, luckily for me, a great friend of mine, who knew the rector of St James's, offered me accommodation there. So I got a very delightful little flat at the top of the rectory. I couldn't have been in a more central place than St James's Piccadilly. It's a very lively community, full of movement all the time and it's so central for people to come and see me, easy to connect up with the main line stations, to travel to the airport and so on. Of course, I'm independent as I'm not part of the staff at St James's so I don't have to be there every Sunday. So I get the best of both worlds.

I knew, of course, when I got back to London that I would be the President of the Anti-Apartheid Movement in reality instead of just on paper, but I didn't realise how quickly I would get involved in the struggle within South Africa. Within a year of my arrival in London, it was announced that the Prime Minister was inviting President Botha to visit. Chancellor Kohl and various others had also invited him – but she had invited him to talk with her about his plans for the reform of apartheid – which of course were no reforms at all. What they were, in fact, was the promulgation of a constitution which provided a tri-cameral legislature of three houses, one for the white minority, one for the Asian minority and one for the Coloured minority, and none for the African majority.

I got an appointment with the Prime Minister before Botha's arrival. I am bound to say she was really quite generous with her time. She was very busy because there was a major miners' strike on and I remember her coming into 10 Downing Street in a fury because she had met some of the pickets on the way. However, we settled down with a cup of tea and I was able to talk very freely about my experience in South Africa. I said to her, 'You know, I'm not talking about Nelson Mandela and Oliver Tambo as if they were symbolic figures; they are my friends and I'm just not prepared to accept that this situation should go on indefinitely.' She then said, 'Well, how would you end it, and when and how do you think apartheid will end?' I said, 'As to when, we ought to have done it years ago; it's not a matter of tomorrow even. But, as to how, we do it by an effective sanctions policy.' She challenged me on the issue of sanctions. And I was able to say to her that the only effective way of bringing apartheid to an end is by sanctions. To which she replied as usual, 'Sanctions don't work.' I said 'Prime Minister, it's very strange

for you to say that because two years ago you went to war with Argentina over the Falklands and the very first thing you asked for was sanctions. And you got them rather reluctantly from the United States of America (USA) and from the European Economic Community (EEC) and the Commonwealth. How come sanctions don't work if you yourself asked for them?' 'Oh,' she said, 'that was a war situation.' I said, 'Isn't there a war situation in South Africa where you have a whole country – Namibia – occupied illegally by 100,000 troops from South Africa for ten years? When you have them marching into Angola and occupying a province, bombing towns in Zimbabwe and Botswana and Zambia, is that not a war situation?' We didn't get any further, needless to say, but her position on sanctions has remained unaltered and so has mine, because looking back I see it has been the use of various forms of sanctions that has been the one effective means of focusing world attention on apartheid as a moral challenge – and that's what sanctions are all about. Sanctions aren't an end in themselves; sanctions are for the purpose of bringing to an end and totally destroying apartheid by putting maximum pressure on the South African government – not on the South African people, on the South African government – and that is what Mrs Thatcher refuses to recognise.

In 1986, after the Nassau meeting of the heads of the Commonwealth, the Eminent Persons Group (EPG) was set up, which was a Commonwealth group representing, through seven distinguished public figures, the whole Commonwealth. I thought, and I think most other people thought, that this wouldn't achieve very much because it was just another group, but in fact it achieved far more than we ever dreamed it could. I had a great deal to do at that time with Sir Shridath Ramphal, then Secretary General of the Commonwealth, because he was responsible for the EPG. This gave us an opportunity to bring home to people in this country the fact that Britain was isolated in the Commonwealth on the issue of sanctions, that, unanimously, the rest of the Commonwealth voted for an effective sanctions policy with only Mrs Thatcher and her government standing in the way. We were bound to go on keeping up the pressure on the government. Not that it was very fruitful in this instance, nevertheless it's something that I will continue to try and do. I've had more interviews than I care to remember with the Foreign Secretary on this same issue. Nevertheless, the EPG laid down a programme which, if it had been followed, could have been the first major advance towards the end of apartheid. It was based on the fact that the white minority would not give up voluntarily its domination inside South Africa. This would only come about through pressure from outside forcing them to get round the conference table. Even Mrs Thatcher had to concede certain very limited sanctions. The EPG perspective had its impact on the USA as well because the US banks came in and Congress opposed President Reagan's policy of so-called 'constructive engagement' with Pretoria. And so it widened the whole international field. I found myself having to go across to the USA to talk about disinvestment in universities, even on Wall Street. This was a very important part of the job and very soon I found that my journeys overseas really amounted to visits to governments, particularly

General Obasanjo, Shridath Ramphal and Malcolm Fraser

Commonwealth governments, to try to persuade them, if they needed persuading, to put more pressure to get a change over the policy of mandatory economic sanctions, under the United Nations.

So, recently, I've been twice to India, where of course I found enormous support from Rajiv Gandhi. I've been to Australia two or three times and, again, from the government there we've had massive support. And so it's gone on. But it has meant of course that the job of President of the AAM has become, I might say, almost a full time job. It would be full-time, except that there are other jobs to do connected with the whole issue. As I said before, I am President of the Britain-Tanzania society – Tanzania being a Front Line State and President Nyerere, as he then was, being really the voice of the Front Line States for about the last twenty years, ever since he became Head of State there. So I've been around the Front Line States; I think I've been to every one except Angola. Really my job is an international job as far as the struggle is concerned.

With Rajiv Ghandi

The President of the ANC, Oliver Tambo, has been a very close friend, I suppose my closest friend in Africa, for more than 40 years. When I went off to Tanzania in 1960 he had just come abroad in order to organise the ANC worldwide, in order to get the whole thing on a proper footing. And his achievement has never had the respect and encouragement that it ought to have had, because he has had to carry the main burden all through those years. He's had to be separated from his wife and family, and for the first ten to fifteen years he didn't get much support. It was only through his steady persistence that he built up a reputation for and with the ANC, which is now of course well established. It is now a 'government in exile' and that is almost all Oliver's work and I really do want to express this because he certainly deserves all the recognition that can be given.

With Oliver Tambo, London, 1960

Oliver Tambo and Andimba Toivo Ja Toivo celebrate Huddleston's 75th birthday

133

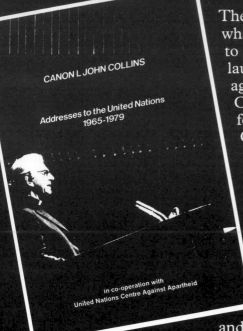

CANON L. JOHN COLLINS

Addresses to the United Nations
1965-1979

in co-operation with
United Nations Centre Against Apartheid

The AAM is a very high profile movement – it's clear what it stands for and there has never been any attempt to be anything but a very high profile movement, launching mass rallies and promoting the whole battle against apartheid in every conceivable way. I am also Chairman of the International Defence and Aid Fund for Southern Africa (IDAF), which was founded by Canon John Collins over twenty years ago. That has as its objectives three things: first of all, to ensure the defence in the courts of political prisoners; secondly, to aid their families; and thirdly, to keep the conscience of the world alive by publications, by every conceivable means of communication. Now that, of course, in one sense, had to be a low profile organisation simply because it was banned inside South Africa for 24 years and anyone proved to have received funds through it was automatically criminalised. The work of IDAF is absolutely vital work and we have the task of raising millions in order to see that the work goes on, and that all those inside South Africa who need legal defence get it.

RIVONIA TRIAL

DEFENCE & AID FUND
CHRISTIAN ACTION
2 AMEN COURT, LONDON, E.C.4

NELSON MANDELA
THE STRUGGLE IS MY LIFE
IDAF PUBLICATIONS

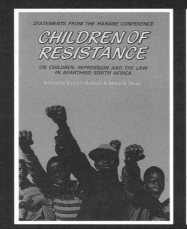

STATEMENTS FROM THE HARARE CONFERENCE
CHILDREN OF RESISTANCE
ON CHILDREN, REPRESSION AND THE LAW
IN APARTHEID SOUTH AFRICA
Edited by Victoria Brittain & Abdul S. Minty

This is NAMIBIA
A PICTORIAL INTRODUCTION

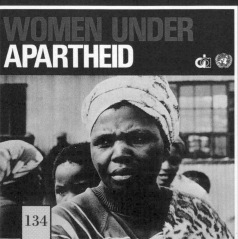

WOMEN UNDER APARTHEID

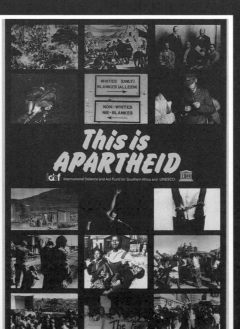

This is APARTHEID
idaf International Defence and Aid Fund for Southern Africa and UNESCO

MAKHALIPILE
THE DAUNTLESS ONE

ARCHBISHOP TREVOR HUDDLESTON
His Life and Work

With Glenys Kinnock at the launch of the International Conference on Children, Repression and the Law in Apartheid South Africa, Harare, 1987.

(l to r) Beyers Naude, Angela Davis, Professor Reg Austin, President O. R. Tambo.

As I said earlier, I had the honour of being the first to propose a cultural boycott, cultural sanctions, and I did it as long ago as 1955. I urged a total cultural boycott of South Africa. The cultural boycott spread and spread and became a really powerful instrument for isolating the South African regime from the rest of the world.

It was supported strongly and out of it grew the sports boycott which, I suppose, in some ways has been the most popular boycott because sport is a most popular thing. Everybody knows that now South Africa is isolated from world sport in a very big way, it is desperate to get back into that field.

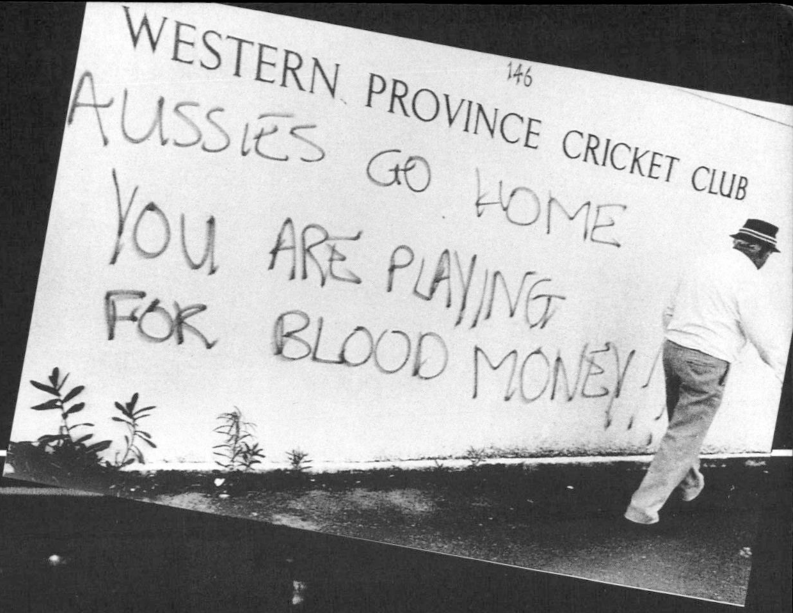

WESTERN PROVINCE CRICKET CLUB

146

AUSSIES GO HOME YOU ARE PLAYING FOR BLOOD MONEY!

APARTHEID isn't SPORT

BANTU-STANS

JOB RESERVATION

358

211
S.A. 1977

357

REPRESSION

PASS LAWS

NO APARTHEID SPORT

137

STOP APARTHEID'S BLOODSTAINED COAL!

BRITAIN DIRECTLY IMPORTS OVER 1 MILLION TONNES OF SOUTH AFRICAN COAL *EVERY* YEAR.
800 MINERS ARE KILLED *EVERY* YEAR IN APARTHEID'S MINES.

But the most important sanction is economic and this, as I said, was recommended by the EPG and supported to various degrees by the US Congress and others. And so sanctions have begun to bite quite severely into the South African economy. Nevertheless, Great Britain continues to invest in South Africa and to trade with South Africa, in spite of the recommendations of the EPG, in spite of our isolation in this way. It's not the only country that does, of course: the Federal Republic of Germany does the same, France does the same, and Israel does the same. Nevertheless, Britain has got the longest history of total commitment to South Africa economically, so we have never let up on the battle to bring about sanctions here.

cape

BRITISH INVESTMENT

One of the most important sanctions which we haven't yet been able to achieve is the sanction against gold, and that involves, of course, the country where the banks are all important in that respect. Switzerland is the centre of that particular trade. And so, not long ago, I went to quite an extraordinary meeting in Zurich. I've been to various shareholders' meetings in Britain but at the Zurich meeting there were over 2,500 individual shareholders! It was a meeting addressed by the president and he had all his directors on the platform and an enormous TV screen above his head, so that his face could be magnified twenty times, and he controlled the meeting from beginning to end. As I had a share I had my name put down to speak. Well, I got away with it for about ten minutes. When I was heckled half way through, I'm bound to say in fairness that he stood up and said, 'No, we must hear him out.' But when I came to the real crux of the matter which was to say that dealing with South Africa in the way the Swiss banks were doing was immoral, then the chopper came down. He shouted at me to stop speaking at once, as Switzerland had diplomatic relations with South Africa. I replied that Britain also had diplomatic relations with South Africa but that didn't stop me speaking there. However he switched the microphone off and then showed a very tendentious film on the TV screen which showed only those blacks and whites who opposed sanctions. He then told the audience that this was the true voice of South Africa.

139

So the question of sanctions has been a very major issue and it's been backed up in our case by massive rallies which have had much bigger consequences than just focusing on sanctions. We had one a few years ago on Clapham Common which was attended by more than

a hundred thousand people. Even the underground railway stations came to a halt because there were too many people pouring through them. We had a great mass concert there, which was a multi cultural affair with people like Hugh Masekela and other great groups like Spandau Ballet who were prepared to support us. It was a marvellous day, very hot with a picnic atmosphere, and I had to address this massive crowd. It's always very difficult when people are really enjoying the

music to know how you break in and how you get them to just pause for a second to listen to the message. But they've always been very responsive, I must say. And then, of course, in 1988 we were focusing on the release of Nelson Mandela for his 70th birthday. And there we had two great events in London. We had the Mandela concert at Wembley stadium which was televised worldwide and I am told about a billion people saw it or heard it. I was there and so was Oliver Tambo as were many others.

And so many great pop stars of the world gave their services. This was not a fund-raising effort – it was very specifically to focus on Mandela, to focus on the release of all political prisoners and on an effective sanctions policy to persuade or to convince the South African regime that it wouldn't get away with it.

We also had a rally in Hyde Park and Archbishop Tutu spoke at that one, as I did too, and that was even bigger than the one on Clapham Common. So having a definite goal to isolate the Pretoria regime, and to do so by means of an effective sanctions policy while reaching out to the mass of people, particularly the young, has been our objective. And I don't think we are doing too badly. Sometimes people ask me what the AAM has achieved after thirty years and I can say that it has made apartheid known worldwide as something basically evil, which cannot be reformed, which has got to be destroyed. I'm certain I speak for the majority of the world's population when I say that that message has been taken in.

141

Only the other day I spent a week in Nigeria and I've never ever had such a reception in any country, African or otherwise, an official reception sponsored by the government. At every place that I went to we got massive support. So one is comforted by that, although I'm not too comforted because still apartheid goes on and we've got to end it.

APARTHEID IS BLASPHEMY
—Archbishop Huddleston

VISITING Archbishop Trevor Huddleston, has described apartheid as 'blasphemy'.

He said this in an acceptance speech after being conferred with the national honour of Grand Commander of the Order of the Niger (GCON) by President Ibrahim Babangida, at Dodan Barracks yesterday.

Archbishop Huddleston, who is president of Britain's Anti-Apartheid Movement, said 'apartheid is fundamentally evil. It cannot be reformed, it is contrary to the will of God. It is an assault on human dignity. It is a blasphemy'.

He said that apartheid was still flourishing in South Africa because the international community had not deemed it fit to deploy a powerful force to the racist enclave.

He said that Britain in particular would remain condemned by history as one nation which failed to confront the evil of apartheid when it actually had the wherewithal to do so.

He said that he had held his conviction against apartheid for 40 years based on his personal experience of the system and not as a result of any academic studies.

Archbishop Huddleston urged the international community to throw its weight behind the current peace process for the independence of Namibia, saying that its success would be a major achievement in the struggle against apartheid.

In giving the award, President Babangida said that it was in recognition of Archbishop Huddleston's 'steadfast and outstanding contributions to the international campaign against the apartheid regime in South Africa'.

In a citation, the Federal Government commended the archbishop for his 'unrelen-

See Page 3 Col. 1

President Babangida decorating Archbishop Huddleston with the national honour. Photo: AKINOLA ARIYO.

142